# Forecast

ALSO BY JOHN PASS

*The Hour's Acropolis* (1991)
*Radical Innocence* (1994)
*Water Stair* (2000)
*Stumbling in the Bloom* (2005)
*crawlspace* (2011)

# Forecast

SELECTED EARLY POEMS (1970–1990)

## John Pass

HARBOUR
PUBLISHING

**Harbour Publishing Co. Ltd.**
P.O. Box 219, Madeira Park, BC, V0N 2H0
www.harbourpublishing.com

Cover design by Anna Comfort O'Keeffe
Text design by Mary White
Printed and bound in Canada

Harbour Publishing acknowledges the support of the Canada Council for the Arts, which last year invested $157 million to bring the arts to Canadians throughout the country. We also gratefully acknowledge financial support from the Government of Canada through the Canada Book Fund and from the Province of British Columbia through the BC Arts Council and the Book Publishing Tax Credit.

Cataloguing data available from Library and Archives Canada
ISBN 978-1-55017-731-2 (paper)
ISBN 978-1-55017-732-9 (ebook)

*to my wife, children, grandchildren, and yes,*
*to you, dear reader—to the worlds and words*
*coming true to us, out of the blue. . .*

# Contents

**BABY SHOUTS DAO**

## Preface

The poems in this book are selected from work written in the 1970s and '80s that was published in small literary journals, in long out of print chapbooks and in my first full-length trade-edition book in 1984. With the sudden demise/restructuring of its publisher, the original Coach House Press, that first book went out of print nearly as quickly as its shorter predecessors.

My initial step toward the recovery of work from this period was to put together, with Joe Denham's invaluable help, a collection of the original chapbooks along with reassembled sequences of poems previously scattered or miscellaneous. We created what I wanted—a definitive, comprehensive compilation—but the resulting manuscript of 350-plus pages proved too unwieldy (or, more generously, untimely) for publication. My attachment to the sequence/chapbook format remains. I've always composed in poem sequences, within which independent lyric instances are often simultaneous pixilation of a more complex thematic constellation. An ultimate assessment of my work would depend upon a reading of these poems in their originally intended contexts, but here I'm reconciled to the more practical alternative of a selection that is representative of my early impulses and excursions.

I'm grateful to my editors at Harbour who proposed this general approach to the manuscript, with the suggestion that I retain one sequence, "An Arbitrary Dictionary," in its entirety. I'd found that sequence, with its paradoxically arbitrary and random formal elements, impossible to select from. I'd sought help from Susan Zimmerman, friend and generous reader of my work since the mid-sixties, and she seemed similarly stymied. There are poems within the "Dictionary" that are better than others, no doubt, but the delights and dilemmas of the stressed form, the evolving argument with the form that becomes an essential element of content, means the best poems are better within the context of the whole, are less if not next to their sometimes lesser companions.

The order of poems in *Forecast* is roughly chronological, although the book's opening sections spanning the seventies are thematically inflected to trace early engagements with place/landscape ("Taking Place"), people ("Ordinary Love") and eros ("The Crosstown Bus"). These strands are not readily disentangled, nor should they be, and of course there are others. Glimpsed there, for example, but not fully stitched into pattern until "An Arbitrary Dictionary," is an articulated engagement with the strictures and opportunities of language.

The most straightforwardly "selected" section in the book is "Baby Shouts Dao," with the poems selected from the original sequence, and presented (beyond the omissions) in their original order. (An interesting exception is the book's title poem, "Forecast," which certainly belongs in "Baby Shouts Dao" but was written shortly after the sequence's first publication.) The late eighties I devoted mostly to writing *The Hour's Acropolis* (1991). As that book and the four I've published since are still in print, *Forecast*'s final section is a selection of miscellaneous poems from the late eighties extending just into the next decade with "When I Heard the Learned Deconstructionist" written in '90, and "Calling" in the spring of '91.

Poetry is prophetic in its attunement to constancy, rather than in any facility with fortune-telling. Its best *forecasts* can feel as familiar and intangible as experience itself—fleeting, glimpsed, sometimes even *wordless,* as the title poem discovers. . . Despite those pitfalls, poems continue to find footing, to discover us dancing, in the sparkly, slippery terrain of language. If the future has room for our mammalian presence, my best guess is we'll keep on walking/despoiling byways of the Milky Way in some awe and much ignorance, with little clue as to destination, with no better guides than our children. My greatest surprise in retrospect is to see how ambivalent I was in my own youth toward the *building* (in every sense) of my life—how hesitantly I came to embrace the mundane, precarious, exhilarating work that has shaped it. Wisdom in an uncertain world? An excess of caution? I came of age in a society devolving into conformity and anxiety, but British Columbia's southwest coast felt simultaneously timeless, gorgeous, spacious—a lagoon of potentiality welled within wild borders of vast geography, unopened history—and my path was lit with the time's late flare of Romantic idealism and Modernist authority. I'm content with these poems today insofar as they're tracking us (from my locales, my love story) as best I could in their idiom and era. They still carry me forward. I hope you will feel in them an ongoing, companionable presence.

# TAKING PLACE

## Debussy Dream

Wordsworth, rower
I see you in this summer
in our open water, adrift

or urging your stolen dinghy
toward the same dark shore—
the sea in fretful, fearful swell
around you and the moods of the moon

and this time there is no abrupt
turning, no escape but
billowed grey-white morning, calm

as you stand, oars loose
and thought askew, as

you pull at the ribs of God
to make your way
to find a channel
around the hard high head-

land, through
to the lagoon, a lagoon
still and quiet in that sea
where stars have faded.

## Nudists at Wreck Beach

They are at the edge
sudden as spring sunshine
testing the salt water with their new
skin. Some are this kind
of animal for the first
time, arrogant with stances
sea-gazing or on their stomachs
near driftwood or clothing.
Their conversation finds cops
and cameras in all cloth.

Others are as old as summer—
slow gatherers of wood and sun.
They smoke and curl
in a luxury of sand, meet every
movement of eye and sea with ease.

And when the public comes
to the public beaches they
are strangers, can claim
nothing but sand shaken
from shoes and shorts, sticky
crotches and cans and glass
they bring with them. Where
once man was a picnic on
a blanket between the sights now
he is spread strangely. There

is no scenery. The tourists
cannot put their eyes
anywhere.

## A Simple Solution

I like to move
in no direction
circulate on rock
by sea

hands spun out in air
to grasp          well
nothing's there

except to hold love's
orbit through this ocean. . .

So all things do
that sense the earth be
round, the fact a circle

and return.

## Overseas

*for Dulce*

A short deception. For a month or two
we make distinctions: the design
of bus seats (here they are covered
like settees) the narrow roads
the many bakeries and butcher shops.

Fresh-killed hares hung from iron
hooks above the street at first seem
ethnic colour. Their rigid mouths
bleeding into bags, white plastic

could have been a clue;
when the money's comprehended
it's the same place, nearly.

You dare it first.
I'm busy still with Cornish walls
called hedges, the thin slates leaned
precariously on the edge in double rows
earth-filled between—a long stability
in this balancing construction.
Three hundred years they've stood
grown trees on them

but along the cliffs to Mevagissey
as the wind rips bits of straw
from the worn hills across the curling water,
as we watch a squall develop on the sea,

you tell me it is not so safe
so small here
as we imagined

and the distance overseas
diminishes, makes room

## The Jewel Tower, Westminster

In the vaults we are
kept moving, rotated
past the treasure.

> This is our heritage; the glass
> shields cultivated pearl
> and crafted stone—

> a clear-cut history. The deeds
> of men are not so brilliant

nor accessible as these
girthed in the endless round
of shuffling feet, the garbled
voices of instruction and
the prodding guards.

Every inch and instant open
to electric eyes. At night

there is a perfect seal:
our crown.

## Farm Sale in Wales

We approach between blackberry hedges
and fine oaks. The old Welshman driving
anticipates a mansion, the last large farm
to fail here, young farmhands doled to city pubs.

Steered from the thicket's lane
and stone walls, suddenly in the open—
old machinery in rows. Grass
wool-thick attests the enclosure
of sheep. Their auction

has attracted tweedy caps and jackets.
The men in them lean at random
on polished walking sticks
as at ease, as inappropriate
as the good weather.
They smoke awaiting

the auctioneer's sharp music.
A tractor starts and stalls.
Boys wrestle and run their red jerseys
ablaze across the green. A lunch van
from Llandovery sells tea and porkpies

and eventually it's done. Farm wives patient
near the cattle trough disperse. A wheelbarrow
and a sheepdog sold with all the rest
are pulled away. In a farmer's van

we share our going
with a ewe, her feet
twine-tied, the rapid
rhythm of her heartbeat
against the metal floor,
a white corner of eye.

## Dynasty

What did you begin here
Muhammad al-Ahmar
beneath the white mountain?

    Marble for our worn soles
    *los Americanos*, blistered,
    scuffed against the history
    of heaven, estranged
    and hitching into it, your

Alhambra, palace of cold fountains, palace
of the cypress, tall prisoner of Spanish cemeteries
once trimmed to your geometry.

In the dust of Ferdinand's invasion
where the Darro and the Genil merge
beneath the crimson shadow of the cross
we linger near the gaping walls at evening

and await a sigh, a whisper
or the screams of sons newborn
from your stone bed, unsprung
inside the filigree inscription:

    *Allah is the only god*
    *There is no god but Allah*

a murmur
        as of gentle water
to turn the olive and the Catholic sun
a thousand seasons.

## Renaissance

Behind the Madonnas and the Saints
the monumental clutter of the centuries
finally it's the landscape the eye moves to—

a refuge, a vestige of Florentine hills
evergreen surviving marble
and metropolis.

## Kernow

*for the movement*

they take the path
repeatedly, once coastal
it becomes
a road, turns inland
sheltered, and the capital
is there, at centre
defended from the sea

    Truro, first a river port
    then mining, more appropriate
    dug to heart the middle ground

and on the cliffs, Lamledra
I am distracted from those edges
in a like direction, find
myself afield through
standing straw and bramble
knee-high

      I wear the seeds, stop
moving, know the earth
unbroken, stone
root-haunted

as on that other rim, Pacific
Vancouver balanced with his ships
and returned to England, nameless.

**The Crossing**

here the star, the far shore
or this tree.  we enter with attention

    what passes and must pass
    to bring us closer

    the ocean heals behind the ship
    the trodden brush springs back

and we are nothing if not impulse to direction

    destination, goal:
    the all of our going

the journals and accounts are no accounting
there is too much to become to get it right

tonight, around the fire
in the heat of all the urgency
to move, waiting for the first
light

    what do we finally write
    what have we always written

    *today we saw two bear*
    *and would have shot them,*
    *they passed so fearfully close,*
    *had the rain not damped our powder. . .*

            and so it goes
        behind us
at a loss for words

not until arrival does the journey
focus.  but that is late and looking
back distorts the purpose

we cannot hold our coming through the world

## The Carpet

on park grass
between ocean
and the city

rolled out
in a noon hour

between the history
and the archives

where we will put our feet
on a floor in Kitsilano

rolled out
obvious, the weave
scattered at the edges

    the Major's stories of Vancouver
    scattered, anecdotal in his ninety-third year
    of the CPR, steel stretched to an idea
    *red-route around the world*
    threads of empire.  the city
                  woven into his fantasy
                   in his words Lord Stanley
                   dedicates the park

    *To the use and enjoyment of people of all*
    *colours, creeds and customs for all time*
    *I name thee. . .*

                no records remained, no evidence but
                the requirement of a history
                a carpet, on the forest
                floor, to calm the sea

a history to be contrived
to accommodate.  somewhere to live

for everyone.  inside the language.

## Pacific

no peace.  the storm ensues.

thunder through the Lions Gate
shakes the windows
scares the animals

the dog cowers at my feet

spring rain, a patch of sunshine on the park
fair weather in the south

in northern lakes the rain collects
responsibly, the dams will never break

the woods are orderly
the mountains hold their shape

the lightning instant passes in the cloud.

## Upper Levels

highway. a cut
        above the city
        and the sea

they have cleared
back
this far
        creeks wear at the culverts
        underneath us

overhead, from cliff's edge
the trees lean in
and cast precise shadow

roots cling to shattered boundary
of mountain
        and gasp
        in thinnest air
        from the cliff's face

        small avalanches sift
        against the inside shoulder

## The Embankment

shovelling the earth away
where it has come down

washed and trodden down
a way: the use of water, men and animals
from the level driveway to the sloping orchard

I'm rebuilding the embankment

uncovering the original large rocks
and putting in the place of those few fallen
other rocks, selecting them

writing this I feel what right have I
seldom working with my hands,
to stand as if a counterforce, a builder
against the rush and crumble. . .

I would sooner, knowing myself
and metaphor, and how best to prevail,
relax with the coming down of the soil and water
in a straightforward descent

but something, neither profit
nor recreation, keeps me at it

as lifting up I test
the weight and shape of every stone
to place each one with care to rest
to hold the next

and to hold a trust
in this indulgence, the bearing
of my work upon the sliding world.

## The Path

I'll try to keep it simple, steps
of stone descending from the house
across a corner of the orchard
then down again beneath the farthest
apple tree. I begin to build the path

just as the blossom makes its promises
over my shoulder, the willow sneaking
into leaf. But there's no reason.
I can get to the trees well enough
for what they'll share of flower
and fruit. This work won't get me closer

unless it's in essentials, hard necessity
the jostled rocks encounter
of making new arrangements
with the earth, fact
of a finger bruised
now healing. In the logic
of construction and continuity

and not to deceive, my path lies
confused as surely as the new grass
searching out its crevices and edges.
For all the probability
of being nowhere further on

I continue, keeping to it.

## Periwinkle

As I'm in the thick of it, thinning
the raspberries, wading in to break
down last year's brittle canes,
a winter late but pleased
with myself and my lazy sense
of gardening as it comes to me—

blue tiny flower, this single
periwinkle, alert in its glossy sea
of leaves, tossed up at my careless feet

makes of every unthinking step
an approach, implicit
with threat and preparation.

## Pruning

If I had this to do
for my life
could I do it, suffer

(not to mention
the pain)
my impatience?

Of the dead and the wild
wood chopped and torn away
some reluctant to come down
I drag through the favoured

branches, damaging them.
How can I say what I need
to save? There's the shape

of the tree
and ruthless energy
and the sharp grace of decision
but after all it's guesswork.

And all for promised growth to make
its vulnerable passage
in the air: a faith

I hold
in what I act upon

if not
in what I am.

Except this now, a winter's ache
working out of my shoulders with reaching,
sense pressed to the cutting edge

pressed to the sky.

## Poem Facing the Other Way

Turn the chair around.
There's the wall that knows me. Mauve
as of a summer evening sky, as I painted it.
A yellow broadsheet, *Being Alive*, by Lawrence.

And at my back the city lights,
another clear cold night, empty
as the perfect days that bring them.

Days I fall short in
for all their distant promises.
Falling for the definite:

The polished car.
Fruit neglected in the orchard.

Certain death.

So the wall.
Frayed edge of the carpet.
Objects to keep from other objects
poor part of my love that dreams past them

and comes faltering back
to purpose, to no purpose.

## Lilac

Poet, get it done.
You've been out to the end
of the driveway

time and again. And
for what? An improbable
sweetness, invitation

the earth extends
and the work
misplaces

as certainty: the lilac at last
learning diffidence, achieving
dissolution in the rain.

# ORDINARY LOVE

## A Little Digging

Between the sun's flash
off the sea and the sun's
gleam off the summer house
windows, leaning west

incredibly, these
countless buds
of ornamental cherry
preparing; I envy

each its forthright
aspiration alight
among companions,
a life

precise within
that latticework
of branches pointing out
the blue sky

beneath which I
have come abandoning
my shovel planted
in the dark earth
in the shadow

of my neighbour's fence.

## Sun in the Afternoon
*for my mother*

What birds this sudden brightness introduces
in pursuit, joyous, flashing from tree to tree to
high in the west where my fancy takes them
sharpening the contours of the mountains.

What a clearing in the wake
of all you told us of your Easter,
in the wake of the death the delicate
nuthatch suffered against your window

while you stirred honey
into warm water and searched
the house for an eyedropper.

Perhaps, even now, days later
high in your favourite maples the crows
go on shredding the limp snake you removed
from the driveway to the sprightly grass

hoping it was sleeping only
a little past winter.
No matter

if our sympathies seem futile.
It's the uncounted
proximate deaths
reduce us, shut

us away from feeling.
And your goodness with the best

is of openings, breaks
in the clouds where the birds
come in. And I come in, crowned

with sunlight, surprised again
for the warmth and my eyes and my life.

## The Veil

*for Leslie*

In nebulae of white
plum blossom
snow's not forgotten.

Asters of blossom.
A cold and starry night.

All bright things live
possessed of themselves,
unavailable. None fragrant,
wooing memory.

When the rain comes tempting
pebbles from the newly turned
earth, it will not tempt these.

Stars in the grass
on the branch
in the air.

Loose stitches of the veil.

This chilling air exposes
my fingertips astray
amidst the petals.

I think of your sleeping shoulders.

Twice on subsequent
April nights the wide-eyed
March moon wakes us.

## Ornamental Plum

For those slender shoots,
sprays of white, a fountain
from the old root

I made a poem: the veil.

In an unused
upstairs room the confetti
of petals blows in

through a window left
carelessly open.

I leave them
littering the sills
unswept

on the empty floor.
They show me through

and through, my hand
on the opened door.

## The Warmest Night of the Year

Be personal, and talk to me.
The only speech that keeps us gives

       one person
       to another.

Always it's a matter
of giving in

       within myself
       surrender.

Of going down into the orchard
to see the stars and leaves.
The warmest night of the year!

They are never any closer
but appreciate
           the distance.

This clear and quiet distance
that allows love
in what would pass so far.

For what has so much need
of the separateness of things?

The starlight in the old trees
has it

      in
      for us.

For me, alone
and standing here,
if I am not straightforward

it is because the simplest things
confuse me, cause me pain.

## Trellis

This is support: I tie up
the tendrils of wisteria

to the trellis I've erected
to carry them over

into their proper fullness
of blossom, come August.

And you my love
in your green dress

invest with shape and scent
my emptiness; the arch

your body makes
to grace my life

is all of consequence
I cling to, and of flowering.

Are you so held?
How much of this
can care and
craft assure?

**The Proximity**
        *for Pierre*

You at your corner
of the table suddenly
mad for something, not
simply women, poetry, friends
but an intimacy so far gone

your shouted words
emphatic hand-slaps
on the worn wood, pointed
gestures between the red
and white carnations

demanding it
declare its absence.
You charge me with complacency,
presume to know I can do
so much more. Pierre
I am more, composed:

My small poems
open a moment
close to me

in the light of friendship
in the light of my love
for a woman, in the shaking
light of the candle near
those carnations

and then close, gone out
from intimacy wide
of what was felt, lost
to their sources.

I am not complacent.
I am sane for something.
It leans forward, patient,

confirmed
in what excites
and continues, promises

the world.

## The Fence Is Really Something
*for David, Hope & Pierre*

Our drunken bluster sounding out
affirmation, conviction, agreements
we might take with us

blunders, teaching me again
those few steps from friends'
porches to the ground

are sometimes the best I take
for friendship. I'm too steeped
in essences of paradox
and contradiction to love enough

our monotonous reassurances
and go out looking for substance.
The fence is really something

I can get my hands on feeling
its rough cedar, seeing over
to the houses and the houses
where no-one I will ever know
lives, never knowing me. . .

till my thinking's made of
what the fence is made of—
dead wood I turn my back on
glimpsing that green frond

of cedar suddenly
astir in the wind
in the light from
Hope's window.

## Indications, Seasonally Adjusted

Everything the dollar means
is down, two cents. Costs
and unemployment rose
two points.

The so-called pleasures
of the rich and the so-called
aspirations of the poor
are pointless.

Their lives continue
to hurt them

for purely aesthetic
reasons. I'm sorry
but I can't help

celebrating, coming in
with the fresh-cut long-stem
magnificent white roses, losing
one or two petals only from the heavy
heads on the stairs

the excellent
spring it's been
for buttercups

crows
and roses

and the fine dilemma
that proposes.

## Premise

A kind of dumb
courage or hopeless
persistence sits up, hits
the keys. It wants to write,
wants to rescue these beginnings

: Pruned twigs I was collecting
for kindling sounded
as I broke them up
as if burning

cracks and crackles
the steady rhythm
of my work kept
random
          unpredictable

and working, listening
I saw among those broken
a core of branch
flame-coloured within
the white outer wood.

: David says what he always says
when he comes down here
to the small clearing, sheltered
between high laurel and the bank
overgrown with blackberry bramble

*The times we've sat here*
*talking away. Bright days.*
*Incredible eh. Every time*

*I see the orchard*
*from this perspective*
*the slope seems steeper.*

Somewhere in Plato there is
the statement: Wonder
is the origin of thinking.

We agree there.
When we talk about it
there are long silences.

## Locale

A candle lit
in the empty
Melini bottle

high moon, dark cedar
and Shakespeare's sonnets
singularly beautiful

shimmer between them
an atmosphere intangible
with a feel for context

light in the air
of a summer's eve
where our words are heard
and our eyes meet.

## Old Fixtures

I love old fixtures
for their human history,
for what they show of service
and of patience:

doorknobs turned
under thousands of hands
into the well-known places

night after night
the lamps relit

a graceful tap
adorning ancient porcelain
letting out continually
its comforting drip

           drip

.

## Ordinary Love

Workmen are painting
the railings blue where I stop

the car. I get stuck
at what is.

What was it this morning?
I let you off on the corner.
You were going to work.

I'm going to work
it out, an equation

for the gold light
holding the windows
and beckoning near
the trees. No need

to go out on a limb. . .
it's ordinary love, balancing.

## Apple

Friends in the kitchen
re-reading Pound's translations
of Rihaku.

I've contrived
to keep us there awaiting
the transparent apple's flowering—

last and finest of the bearing trees.

A few days only. Nothing
after a thousand years

for exiles of the Empire hesitant
at the ancient gate. Only beyond
in the garden, that canopy

of fragrance, art's
complement: coincidence.

Friends come home.
There is everything.

# THE CROSSTOWN BUS

## The Lights

The first time I tried
to write, needing to,

it was about the lights.
They were my lights, coming on

in shadow lengthening
along the flank
of the high ridge across

the river.
I remember looking up

the word *caress*
for its spelling.

## The Approach

You turn on the opera
and then go out

to dig at the roots
of the rose
bushes.

Below the skyline
of the city a ship
slides to its berth.

The streets
shining with rain
bend down to meet the sea.

My face is lonely.

How can I step
without asking
into your hands?

## To Orpheus, Turning

What were you thinking of?
Not we would-be singers, desperate men
glancing for centuries over our shoulders
to be sure, our finest music scaled
down to doubt, your moment. Not us
but the known woman, earthbound,
falling back of the singing, a face,
its shadow, farewell.

And so we are abandoned, hanging
breathless on the old strings
tightened to tune

on our every word

and at heel, twisting
on the balls of our feet
on the small bones
of our necks

to be free of the dark route,
rooted to loss and the light's
insistence, while in thicket and city

the maenads squeal
their delight.

## Homage to the Pornographer's Model

I spread you out, a carpet, a catch-all
seductress, the temple's flat
dimension. The sun falls through

the window. No-one is watching.
On my knees on my ass I go

down for you, for what my want
can make of you, willing flesh
of the photographer's profitable

gloss. For lips (*O lips!*) slickly
rouged and pouting, meticulous
attention to angle

and lighting, to piquancies
of dress, undress

and for this engaging illusion—
you are no more nor less elusive
than a real woman—

       The proposition was
that I do everything. When I turn
the page after coming so close
there's nothing between us

but my little death, *ma petite
tristesse*. My wet tissue.

## An Empty Glass

Considering the hopelessness
of useful things: a favourite chair
anticipating posture, an empty glass
to be washed and refilled, each hole
of the telephone dial returning
to its predetermined digit. . .

Considering the helplessness
of useless things, moonlight
on granite or water
under the bridge,
the return of mist
to the river, the return
of the lovers the morning after. . .

I'd like to throw everything
out the window. Imagine

my grandfather's rosewood writing desk
in splinters, this typewriter shattered,
the strung out telephone buzzing
busy for joy, strewn books
swollen and wrinkling
in the damp air.

What a museum.

Moonlight, come
sit with me awhile.
Mist get a grip on the sad
stonework, let go of the sliding river.

Lovers, for love's sake, cross over.

## Reclined, at Speed

By car from California
reclined, at speed
in the cold

is just the sleep to fold
out this insignia the poem
pins on as a man cast
in a circle.

Never event redemptive
of his bland bronze.
Never resolution.
Not even enigma enough to tune
a fascination.

Beneath this sign find only
my memory for the dead
and ordinary question:

was there once a natural
grace, an ease and instinct
under the trees not circumspect
not intersected by furious highways?

Rolled through the land cut open
his stance is becoming, spear-thrower
poised at the reach of some thrust,
some anger I dream for. Absurd
in the metal's grip
to threaten

driving
the same point home
against hope, against
the window, snow

blurring.

## The Crosstown Bus

I'd forgotten how dark the city
from the empty fluorescent bus

and how warm the dark upon
stepping down. As a young man

I'd walk with a young man's arrogance
sure you'd be at the party, picking up

your scent already on the expectant
air. You'd be there ahead of me a little

on Pine Street, leading me on, the music
behind us, before I knew your name.

## Theresa

In these, our first
few hours, deliciously
wet with each other
I believe in everything

I've ever believed in
and loved best
and as well: your eyes,

hair, body in my hands,
beautiful mouth, murmurs
of pleasure. Theresa, you.

## An Apprehension

As we walked I bent down
to tie my shoelace and smelled
pungent blossom, an apprehension
of May in February. I stood up

beside you in the warm darkness
and we turned around together
to locate it.

It was by a low rock wall
on an ascending curve of roadway:
either the one that ended
and we turned back

or the one that went up
and over the hill
and home.

## May and Memorial

I've just thought, comfortably
of making love to you
some warm spring evening

among the graves.
At the corner

of May and Memorial
there is a house we could live in
with low bright windows reflecting

the cemetery, mooning
those sun-long avenues.

A red setter crosses the street to me.

Under scratchy pines
reading the markers, across
the soft level ground I go

all the way down
to the sea to sit

on the lip of the wall.

## Riddle

A turn of phrase or feeling
between us as we drift
down the Seine acknowledging
we can't get along. For my part

afraid to be in Paris alone
or home outside our advertised
future, awash in the loss

of everything passion proposes,
cowardly, heroic, I take to heart

after the stretch of flat water,
empty sky, numb historic presences
looming—promise of a private, honest
life, your eyes

bright with tears over couscous,
our mysterious vows, consolations.

## For My Wife of 27 Days

We spoke our vows, each chosen
word into the public air
resounding.

They are behind
and ahead of us, a far
perimeter, background, hollow gong
unrung yet by our full-swung lives.

Only our sounding, for decades
will fulfill them.

Tonight, alone
grieving an old love
a small, sweet, unspecific song
is suddenly alive in me
as my sobs subside

as though spring were come
in this surprisingly warm
November rain, composing

our prelude
out of soft sky
out of nothing.

## A Devotion

You are the dream I conjured
from silence, out of hearing.

We danced once.
A nod from your mother and we're on our way
in the Volkswagen, your young son strapped
sideways in the narrow rear seat. The ride

made the time I needed to sing your praises
again, to praise your beauty against your mild
denial, against the years. I'd meant to take my car

but now must get back from your place
on the Crosstown bus, if it runs this late.

If it runs at all.

# AN ARBITRARY DICTIONARY

*to Penelope Connell*

*whose dictionary it was*
*fell open*
*to the first word*

## Thorough

Off we go into
the park. Around
near the zoo. A loop.

Alley-oop. Take the brake
off. At the testing station
they give it a pull
and a warning.

Through and through.
Moss and mold work the old
wood. It smells true.

Troughs of the eaves
fill. Furrows, path-side
awash. Stop for coffee.

Park in gear
going everywhere.

## Fret

Oh Thoreau.
December on your calendar
for which they chose
a wintry sunset
and the quote:

*If you have built castles in the air*
*your work need not be lost; there*
*is where they should be. Now*
*put foundations under them.*

Of some Castilian woe, notes
to the latticed interior
light. To play out anxiety:

fingers flayed and railings.
Railings! Weep guitar.
Each tear's tiny erosion
home against the keystone.

Go not to Lethe, those waste waters.
Prose is prose is prose.
Float the morning rose.

Throw an oar away.

## Scale

Chanted descent
of the seconds
to 1980. The year
in lights on the TV.
Gold foil peeled
from the last three
chocolate coins.

A balance
of new days.

Sweep and lift of cloud
above Capitol Hill. A fine
mist. Van Morrison's extension
of the old song, *It's All*
*in the Game*

into the music. My love
for you. Everyone's future:

word size.

## Coil

Turned and turned
down

deep
in what I know.
By what means? My own
surely, though unknown

the future twisted
to them—implicated.

Chekhov lit one room, stage-wide. . . .
Though everything of importance
paced urgently outside

it needed a known cage
for full play, a scenery
he could bear to see.

Bear with me, conducive
energy, electric sense

light everything for ecstasy
again, that when her fingers stray

on the old upholstery
inveigling *what's this?*
of me, I may plead more

than *spring* and
*broken*.

## Friary

These words, beloved of the Order
I beg them for, a brotherhood
of syntax to house

continuity: lamps alight along
the stilled corridors, each
place set at the long table.

Of meagre art, such luxuries.
Not these words especially.
I promise myself to any

the book as it falls open
the dream as I'm awoken
play on. They stay home.

## Obtain

Get what is

given (a year
getting clear
of what was

held

dear) Dear heart:
I want you to know.

What holds! Deep
sea-going. Old
fridge full of sour

cold air. And sweet
breathing as you read
in the sun in your chair

at home in the spacious room.

## Solitaire

Working back
through red and black
(passion, hard fact) patience
(a real gem in the cards)

lets Kings and Queens and Knaves go
down past deuce to zero: bare bulb
above the typewriter. Show it off

or wear it well
it's one

wordless hint
and brilliant ringing

at an ear
or of the proffered
hungry fingers

one ascribes words to.

## Consistence

The yogurt thickens
in the warm oven

as does this
domestic bliss

and boredom
we, of all lovers
(as all lovers)

lust and learn for
least. Between

the glass jar
and the pure
sustenance

you note a clear
and liquid
envelope and lack

of adhesion
you delight in.

## Deadly

In -earnest
what source
brightening

the blank sky, swath
of water under, searches

me out, idly
wanting a word?
This one now! How
begun with whatever
resolve, to go on?

-accuracy only
can enliven song.

-haste dissembles
it's the sun. I stare

at the yellow
typing paper
hoping to go one

better.

## Harpy

So greedy am I
for my vital soul
I neglect the scavenger
crone in me (sticky stutter

of unhinged wings) trying
her claws in the rind

of each aspiration, all
whole rhyme, every confidence

the thing can be known
not hideous before it's flown.

## Tariff

Yes. Again. Young limb of plum

hung over me, grace
of a momentary sadness
and wisdom.

Trees spaced nicely

standing around—
I hate my feet, speech,
gesture, digestive processes—

the whole outgoing mess of me

not for the spatial disruption—
for the wasted motion
taxed and awkward

                      carrying over

second by second
year by year
of first things.

## Bite

Hand that feeds me
hands that feel me
I hate hurt
but need distinction.

Okay, cut the sods away.
Rocks under the lawn.

Handled properly

they defy description—
chintzy tourist
of the bland illusion
there's somewhere to be
and tons to see.

Even my wife has stories

wherein we
are the dullest
detail, fully realized

beings eye-wise
with an ear for prose.
It's a tyranny. Lady
aglow in your skin

dig in.
Let's spring the main thing.
Wheel away a yard
or two and feel the weight

of feeling for you, free

for friend, incisive word.

## Pup

Out under the sun in spring
things seen, known, solved,
remembered only, all

come up again: issue
and solace of the world.

Roll over, play ahead.
new tricks for old.
I love to nuzzle

you my beauty, all in a tumble
gold green gold green gold.

## Fish

A dozen oysters
count. First

delicacy I devised
for you, fried
lightly in chives
and butter. But more

of your glossology
than mine—lapsed

vegetarian, lips pursed
for the pond's viands,
tiny silver dolphins leaping

on your earlobes, tank-suit
damp over belly, breasts
and behind, a seal

impressed of the water.
I nose about

in aquariums of air, nibbling, fattening,
nearly blind, instinctive. Bright rain
splashes the windows, freshens

your scent. Tang
of April greenery, mint
and fennel. A brush with nettles.

Swim free. Make a meal of me.

## Round

It turns. Loops monotonous

of luxuries, losses.
But circling too, good echoes
become roses again on the scent

of the old song. I mean June
is June. It finds you
or you live that long. That too
a slovenly re-cognition. *Row*

*row, row your boat.* Go outside.
Who can? I've begun to unravel
this morning the morning

glory from the raspberries.
No, to be truthful, finished, days ago
but right now on *unravel*

the ribbon ripped
and only when rewound could I

(ripped) continue. Begun, I want nothing
but this. Words along a line.
A long line

the words snarl. *This?*
*Get serious.* It's something

I can almost do. Maudlin, drunken
precision. The keys jam trying. . .

I have the spine of one
of those plastic binders

and ring the desk lamp then
the window frame. Come in

here on the down-
beat. Sing it again.

## Stage

The play's not the thing
by half. Even unrehearsed
in wit and anger, quick words'

delight sets me hammering
out a construction can hold
me forthright, outspoken.

Subtle carpentry.
Tricks with light.
And underneath, somewhere

the earth
and deeper. I got the garbage out
of the basement, old mattress, boxes

of past girlfriends' stuff, all musty
and lay on the lawn then and thought
of the props and the plot: trees

full of wind and sunlight, wife
full of baby—an intermission
at no-one's peril. Feet first

through the footlights at my own.

## Iconometer

Here's how to find
the view. Don't stare

about blindly. Through
the glass favoured
subjects in their true colours

address you. Take their measure
of isolate beauty: orange tarpaulin
(15 by 20) green tent and blue,
sombre pennant of cloud

at horizon. Forget the eyes' wide
love, impossible masses brightening
everywhere for them. These optics

are your instruments dear monarch, mind

their apportioned care
of the kingdom. Never directly
acknowledge the zenithal sun.

## Question

Whose government of words
are these few: feudal masters

of the plodding stanzas, syllabic
disciplinarians, icons
of restraint

abstraction

promising the long moan
of the silence following
(also theirs) a despair

of stricture, closed mouths?
I raised them high
and by that strategy of fortune

wish them lies, or risen

in our voices otherwise, aspects
of full governance, graces

of ourselves.

## Calkin

The danger's a pedestrian
half-heartedness persistently afoot

on the turned-down edges
of good fortune.

Steel toe, heavy
leather, good

ankle support—
you can hardly feel

the ups and downs over
protruding rock

and insidious stumps
of small alder

before they sprout
again, giving warning.

That's the going assumption.
Sit and kick

at the swordfern and bright bracken
in the half light.

Drive right away in runners.

## Race

To what end? A start
in the dark—for us then

shy with lust
and baby though nameless
running late already.
That last minute rush

for the first ferry, 7:40 AM
for Langdale. No illusions.
Portent

is a forward chunk
of natural development
flashing past. A new reach
of branch over
                    the eaves
was just that

the birch is bigger.
It doesn't want us

to stop. The past flashes
its traffic lights over
those go-ahead all-clear lunges
you loved out from under
the gun, but here

pace these
few acres of sun on the water.
Higher and further it's gone

behind Bowen. Get going.
Let go of my hand.

## Compress

Smaller and
smaller, halved
and quartered
in the folds

made generous
with next to nothing
the last thing holds

a letter. Eh? 'A'
and here applied
real, close, by
hopeful hands:

its mere touch
the exact pressure
that springs them all
to our explosive need.

Into his majority, age-
less, adamant, master
of the caged page, king
to his diminished volumes

this missive strides
and widens wonder with his lies.

## Piper

The tune now man (or god)
none can call
                       till it fall
on the ear from that oblique

and common quiet, where enthralled
we've paid
(the coin the counterpoint we've kept
to old one-step monotony).

Who can think it through
or the moments gone
in symphonic apprehension?

Pandeans, Andeans, Scots et al.
toy no longer.
Play what's promised

in the patient sombre tone
of Ashbery's *Late Echo*
in the sun's tenor
in the mountainous notation

begun by each forever.

## Boot

One of a pair flopped
over on its side, Persi
(for persistence, a cat)

excavates
with quick, extended
paw. Finds fluff—

brown balled-up sock stuff
from the toe

tossed, then the end
of a lace to exhilarate
little jaws and littler lips—
paws bunched, whole body stretched
against the eyelets.

The leather is grey-white
with a fine dust
from the sanding I've been doing

of the old window frames.

## Handsel

*for Forrest*

My gift, the first, before
I thought of it
is the assumption
you will know

as well as I how
the stars go, whose
the new-leaved foxgloves are.
We will have things forever

if not always
to say to each other

no witching in the woods, no woodening
for all its power, can hollow.

## Round

Again! So soon!
Is this to try invention?
Did I presume to make

a progress? I've a chord
or two for you, you elves
of the book's nooks, demons
of the same page. I've a chorus
will smooth your exit, a corner

of the verb, transitive.

Its scaffolding
will keep you young—
strung up with your instruments.

And all those pretty pebbles slung
back in the rough
that grew them.

## Exoteric

Out the open doors past
the unidentified small white flowers
and crescive scent of night-scented stock

we've meat on the fire
and the wine in our heads
of day-wide unread secrets.

## Franciscan

I, whose canticles
are faint praise

hymns to self legion
good works inconsequential

for a few stale Girl Guide cookies
thrown to jays? The challenge

of a word, a name, millennium
of orthodoxy you took up
in flurries of new light

a drama of outward action
and we can blame no history
of systems, superstitions

for our habitual lethargy
of spirit, mummeries
of brotherhood.

I have it whole, somewhere

and when I go
into that tract between
the laurel, wall and apple tree
to know, to say

to hope, approach. . .
it's small and obscure insofar
as I've ignored or cloistered it.

Some leaves, a strand of morning glory
hang, three-cornered, independent
in the half second

I forget to overlook them.
They are yours
who knew the gift

in everything
in everything
our endless debt.

## Withershins

Those rains, our wettest spring
so utterly unwound the sun
by June twenty-second '81

we jeered its fitful glimmer
on the shrubbery, its fatuous fleeting grin
as the next inevitable low swept in.

The smart-ass clocks buzzed on
in their quartz guts; hooves
of the milk cows rotted
in Matsqui.

Every one of the million or so
here called *us* for no good reason
half hungers for, half gulps
(in private, turgid, unhinged moment)

his sloppy, buoyant Waterloo:
torrential dark, a dove.

## Sojourn

Rest here gentle reader
from your labour
and delight—as ill-defined
by now, no doubt, as mine.

We have a few lines yet.
Put up your feet, sit back
and recollect. For though our lives
seem ours alone and less

than comprehended, they thrive
in our arrangements. My father
fifteen years estranged

made an overnight of it, opined
upon the greatness of *The Sound
of Music* and banged on wistful

re some soldiering in Greece, a piece
or two of furniture I grew up with. . .
but not whether I was fair at birth

nor by any measure so admired
as Japanese pedestrians
who never cross against the light.
So you who've read this far

who never knew me, might
as well as any and are welcome
and deserving—family. Breathe easy

sleep well and by your grace read
on, that I may live

and host song briefly in your presence.

## Tuck

No life for a fat man
with that once merry band gone wan
on a diet of personal aggrandizement

and Perrier. Seamless joviality
and the world's best venison
seemed a good glue, tight

as the skin-tight denim
declaration of the waist
that's been taken in, fit
to the loss

of weighty purpose.
But why pretend. I knew him when
I nurtured a fat kid's desperate sense

of justice as revenge, defence
and all those summer friends of surfeit

's equitable redistribution
had more to lose: a sleek
self-righteous adolescence.

## Inequality

Go delude a moralist.
Confound a good man.
The tragic mathematics of justice

unbalance us.
I'd cheat on a metaphor
to get off this level

scaffolding with my head.
I measured every rafter
but the ridge-

beam had a wow in it
I had to allow for.
*That's fuck all*

said the roofer
who missed the pun
but got the job.

## Direct

Denizens of gesture
at my thresholds struggle.
I like that lie. Dramatic.

One for Dr. Overview
asleep in the gods.
Between you and me

were there a point plainly
visible
        we'd come right to it.
It's not words

fail me. Their skies and bedrock,
hurt dumb necessities, reasons to be

are void, filmic, a scenery.

## Figwort

No greenhouse meditation this.
Mere description convinces

Botany's no science
for the subtle soul.
Coarse, garish, stinky plant

I need you ugly as I feel
by abstraction distended to distraction.
Hold my place for me, will you?

If you hadn't come up
in Literature

you'd thrive in this manure.

## Billing

Loves as random
as dissolute finger and blind eye
identify. Constellations

of adorations starring
none. An itemized
account

of prescribed attentions
imposed intimacies?

The dues for this

accrue in the cooing
against that ear
the world turns

from con artists, guess-men
toward some gentle inclination

of her fine head, extravagant
wink of mind.

## Out

It is nothing
but a means of feeling
who you were

before your new condition
becomes you.

A kind of memory.
And nowhere

to go but must be
close to home eventually—

within which trivial distillation
hurt absence is suspended

at a distance
and loss blurred mercifully.

Who'd clear it up
to satisfy one word

when by the time you do slip in unheard
her mood has much improved?

## Afterword

*An Arbitrary Dictionary* was begun of a desire to be writing coupled with a despair of subject. It is arbitrary because the poems' titles, their governors, were selected at random, blindly, appointed perhaps by fate. (My method was to close my eyes, open the *Concise Oxford* and put down a finger.) I felt at first my obligation to be a complete definition of the proffered word in a personal context, a thorough (if idiosyncratic) elucidation. Quickly I came to allow myself a more oblique "take" on many of them: an errant, mischievous (possibly revolutionary) push against their authority, or tyranny. Here and there I have had the sense of being a novice fisherman, learning to play the word with grace and without injury, true to its liveliness and my practice. The risk in all of this is that the words, like anything we love or need, may be less graciously received than taken on; that in the reach for revelation one gets hold only of redemption, or less. The method's reward is in the rich complexities luck and accident lend to language, in the possibilities for responsive and responsible play.

## BABY SHOUTS DAO
*for Forrest & Brendan*

GENESIS 1:10
a notion
an ocean

## First Structure

All day I get in and out
of the hole as the work gets
better by the shovelful, thorough
and rhythmic, the digging returning

a dignity to my muscles slackened
by the half-life of a half-lived
career, a middle age measured
from day one, first

mouthful, proceeding to what I knew
then as needfully as to what I know

will end: hardpan days (as if
given a footing, a foot in
the door, there's no further
but to fill them up

with one shit after another).
You're welcome here
asshole, worst self, confined
by complaint or regularity
to these few cubic feet
of air to be interred

by outbuilding.
But out on the bluff
I've scraped the rock clean
for the sweep of March wind off
the lake, for the whole

valley and Valhalla, skies full
of cedar, mosquito hawks' whirr
of wings, old moons, falls

of snow and long westerly light,
rivulets, ripening mosses, the big

picture, a dwelling.

## Poem for the New World

What's what? Mothers
are mothers and feed

us and upon us. Their moment
is upon us. I thought open-ended

rectangles of pure blue
between the downtown buildings.
I dreamed in neutral on a hill the shift
came away in my hand.

So much world.
So little in it

thought true, said well.
A good push of cloud bunched
over Thurlow at Pendrell catching

the city light when you were two
hours. My son: huge wayward eyes, long fingers—

your mother's mouth, an intricate ear. Feasts
be theirs, and yours to nourish

me, relieved of this meagre miscellany
I sought, sorted and can't abuse.

## Further

No roof yet.
Through the rough opening
framed for double-glazed patio doors

a quarter moon reaches for me, further

than the light that snaps on at such moments
announcing POEM, further than that aging
but excellent idea

of what our effort means, our menial geometries
in the face of diffuse, encompassing heaven—
further even than the week that follows

wallowing in the daily detail threatening
to swallow these words in the making, over
and above everything

her shine comes, shadowing
a star as far as we are.

## The Stars

I lift you up to calm your crying
erase its interruption of my work
and point out rocks and trees, the wild
tiger lilies where our property begins.

You push back your head from side to side
to see it all—shape and colour, or something
even simpler, original

my baby talk won't trick into the open.
When you sleep I look up
from the fire cleansed

of names, any further
attempt at description, all
but the absurdities of range I fathom

laughing a little, amazed
to see them.

## Forrest's Perfect Chuckle

Pure chuckle, laughter's
preceptor, first
person universal

of delight
from the soles
of his size-one booties takes flight

through his knees frog-
kicking glee, tummy's fun-drum
ruckling up and out

to you (if imitation
became me, were I capable. . .)
Santas, sound poets, hysterics

I dare you. Put him up
in the air in your arms
and see

how artless he
makes art's best argument!

## Day Care

A density of affection
when childless I never expected

is atmosphere.
Here we are at daycare

and you must have your airplane
your orange car. You take them along

till I'm taken by them.
The character of objects shifts

in your proximity; trinkets
incidental blips
sing terse avowal

of possession: need and care.
Things everywhere aspire

to be words of yours, loves of mine
extravagant with transport, sky.
At 4 PM I remind you

(clutching a new watercolour
heart set on the yellow tractor

across the road)
to pick them up and bring them home.

## Baby Shouts Dao

Dada at loose ends
in the mansion of his anecdote
can't hammer home

from the piecework
room to room, scraps
of flashing, the last
closet, a good word

for Mum's faraway look
her salal berry pancakes. . .

till baby shouts *dao!*
palms and delivers
the half-dead horsefly

mouths the tiny shiny screw

sits back the wrong way
on his foot tucked under
and hugs the phone.

## I Say What You Say

I slow down
for you

who dash so quickly
from one thing to the next—

rocks you can grasp
from the driveway, scraps

of branch blown down.
*Big tree. Pretty tree.*

I see what you say.
*Water. Road.* Slowed

without time to compose
what we do

in apparent repetition.
*Big truck. B'bye truck.*

Hundreds of times a day
I say what you say

in thoughtless incantation
kept quiet, dumb-

waiter of the big words
ghosting our progress

up the old trail through the alder.
*Mum. House. Okay.*

## Birthday

You're born to me
in this thought of you
I have taking a break

from painting the back rooms
of the new house as I sit
at the table you'll know

one day as the old one.

The view is of some spindly firs
below the house, the little bluff
with its friendly boulder, patches

of yesterday's snow among the salal

and all of us (a family)
but especially you
(no longer at one with your mother)

somewhere out of sight down the driveway.

This celebrates your singularity—
day-bright delineation of who you'll be.
Your sex, hair colour, distinguishing marks
are the easy mysteries, soon solved. . .
When you're fully born

it's this intimation, sudden unsummoned
sense of you

I'll have no more clearly, you'll need
most of me, I'll keep
free as I can.

## Second Son

Among the busy women my hands
are redundant. I stand, expectant
but expendable, a guest
of honour, pawn
of fashion

in the surgical glare, adjacent
to the doctor's command
of the moment, the dignity

of my wife's effort

and you, dragged in naked
swung in the air by your heels
have only to breathe and be perfect. . .

heart-shaped inverted scrotum
with which you surprise

me to tears

for your mother's relief and elation
your manifest connection, mine.

## Entreaty

Courage here—
your eyes' astounding blue, fine hair
(fuzzy in back from rubbing the pillow)
as you pull away, eager

for play, car ride, outside.
Whenever we part I feel it a little—
sentiment scribbling its caricature already
of myself as aging parent pleading

*This may be the last time, you never*
*know.* But true, oh fearfully

possible, inevitable. However it goes

we'll go from here: your grey wool jacket
tugged on just so, loose at the neck, the few
new freckles you count recklessly, my hands
wriggling your runners on. You'll go

however it goes and from my joy in you—

even here, this brilliant April morning

especially here through the clean green colonnades
of young alder, vine maple—dodging away just under the lances
of shadow flashing

asking courage of me
as never I needed nor knew it in sorrow.

## Days in the Dark of Building

Days in the dark of building—
board on board and tile to tile.
A comfort in the tiredness
blinds me; the windows screened
against *no-see-ums* blur the stars

so I can't say
what vision knows—its furthest reach
requires a mind expansive and specific

and mine sighs, *Oh goodnight.*
Or pioneering doggerel sorts out

dog
and cat snuggling on the deck
I built in a blur but sit on

with a view—definite trees—an acreage
to be landscaped—orchard to complement
woodlot. I'll work it for years. For my sons

I've apprehensions, don't care
for legacy, paternal imposition, clay
I felt my father fumble handling me.

But I build, deep-bearing
in fluid bonds gone concrete
a southwest exposure.
I live in it for love

the beauty of my wife in every room
her hands on cups, on sheets, on my shoulders
her heart in the diving flare

of the fuchsia, the corn's late-August
haughtiness, the boys' miraculous breathing
after dark.

## Forecast

Clear days come, empty
my head

for hard ground, crunch
of snow, elemental

light: cutting edge
of moon cresting

Mt. Hallowell as I finish
stacking firewood. Last night
I sat up with a son

whose bronchitis, hoarse
appeals for Mummy eased, easing

the briefest of understandings
between us, wordless

forecast. Tonight
I take his brother out

for the Milky Way, promised
all day but eclipsed

in all this moonlight.
I try to locate something else

of importance up there
as he looks down

at the driveway, rough
with mud chunks and frost-

glitter (disappointed, I think)
till his announcement:

*There's the Milky Way.*
*We're walking on it.*

# CALLING

## And Hold

Days after the wind driving in
to teach I notice

the broken points of the trees, maple
and alder mostly (the conifers strew
branches or go over from their roots)
but these fail where they appeared
strongest, their trunks' sheared

white wood for a few days before the weather
works its grey in
                    mere ghostly fingernails
or sentinel fingers asserting
ascent's deception:

look where we were. A topic this morning

is abortion. So where
does life begin? Birth, conception, a glance
on the street, chance meeting

substance—from endless encounter working

out distinction, definition, legal frame-
work of the good, the policy, program
stillborn

power of the human hold, habits
of mind, heart, history. Do I know

others? Enquiry
along these lines allows none. At break

I get out for some air, step in
to the stress of the emptiness of questions

near a few trees and cars closer
asleep on the gravel.

\* \* \*

Put any tune to any image sequence
and the mind makes concordance, half
the magic of television, whole

history of art: harmony's assumption
taken to heart. Out here I hear

the mantric wince and whine:
our best RV, analysis

       spinning its wheels

gunning the mystic option

of get up alone and go, lure
of the crack of light at the door.
An essential disorder requests

the pleasure. . . no proposition

(not even this) can argue me out
of my body for long. Back inside

the discussion, killing
time, its involuntary system

clenches and flexes on
its way to you whom I imagine

snuggled up warm
and sexy and ready

for anything.

\* \* \*

You welcome me
in tears about the starving

Ethiopians, TV-wise mothers holding up
their children to the cameras, our eyes.

Take them.
Feed them.

The mothers display them, careless
of their own lives, offering

their offspring, putting them
first, their tired arms

holding us up to ourselves, hopeful. . .
the hope for us—a way to care

effectively. You cry and I am quiet.
I think of the journey we're taking

soon to San Francisco, the pleasure
of "the break we deserve

from the children." Any flutter
of apprehension

touches down there near my sons, their faces
and hearts should we fail

to come home. The Ethiopians
are home, starving
by the millions. We see the wheat

arrive, red and white bags
stamped CANADA. Clark emerges

"shaken" from viewing
the CBC footage. We're entitled

to our opinions, entitled
to the dictates of conscience,

to pride in our generosity, shame,
guilt, to turn off

the set, to send a cheque,
to discuss at leisure,
to pity, to cry, to condemn.
We're entitled, as always

(as the mothers offer
their dying children)

to everything. Everything
but their dreadful dignity.

## Rugosa

Here's how I'm reminded
nothing can placate
your loveliness. I turn

on the path to the sea to see you
coming down in dappled light
and ache immediately, the watershed

of instance evident in a sip, slip
of the tongue to sweet
nothings, sigh

of the ruffled ocean, wave
of your body at rest on its side.
Smooth thigh. Milk-pink

rugosas overwhelm
a cedar shrub. Our son

drops his handful of strawberries
on the page. I'll go along

with you to buy the bougainvillea
but it will prove useless.

## Married Love

Of late love it's workout
pushes the pulse rate
our weekly hour

at the Rec Centre, kids at the sitter's
or preschool, us just beginning

the Global programme (medium
weight plus repetition
for endurance). I see the blonde

at seventeen, red swimsuit
cut high on her hips and hear

my habitual whispers groan
and sing, true
to their conditioning
                    but distantly

so much the echo I forget
till writing this to laugh

and smile
remembering your smile
when I joined you in the water

to stroke out together, leisurely
for the deep end (steamy

and quiet)
and back again.

## Shine

(a rhupunt)

Upon my plate
I risk a late
extravagance

hoping your sleep's
not yet so deep
no dream can chance

upon the shine
of oil and wine
and avid glance

to bring you round
to slipping down
your shot-silk pants.

## I Do

My best word's less

than merest daylight
touching you just right.
There. There.

Not caring.

Say love? A nudge—
the barely perceptible

shove suffered learning
to bike ride, swim

lets go but
gives it away, holds
in the air an air

of retraction even
on the cusp of poise, false

buoyancy pedaling some shiny
contraption at odds

with the simpler, serious
light of your skin.

## One. Life

Begin with the windows open, rain
all night long. . .

        Come on
little fella (waist-deep
in momma)

prove me wrong. You did! You do
swan snuffle

at the nipple soon as
your cord's untangled

and sleep
herb-sweet

confounding morning, everyone's
excitement, the calendar's
idle threat and tiresome
enumeration: one

life with her yellow toque on.

*for the birth of Angelica Alba Pass, September 13, 1985*

## Calling

Lady, I'd go out
on a leaf for you, on an edgy

sea. Yes, even short my sex-
tant. *Tant pis.*

I do. Daily go

to the tender tip
to the ends of the earth.
It's an easy step

through the bathroom window
into the addition, the newly framed
bedrooms, children and more

than I'd hoped for single.

The April sun's intense
in the corners and the smell
of fresh-sawn lumber, daffodils
nodding *yes*            (sure enough)

*you'll die,* shouldered aside
on the swell of sad self-pity cresting
a half heartbeat back of great beauty.

Great responsibility. Nearby

you're pricking out tomato seedlings
unable to sacrifice even the feeblest and angry
with that calling, the passive greed

of each for an egg cup
world of its own
however fragile, finite.
There I go

hammer in hand
and this stub of pencil
making it big as I can.

## Sagittarius A West

Let's be precise
in this. We speak of the centre
identified at last

at a distance
of 10,000 parsecs, 20 times as far
as the Great Nebula, almost invisible
due to red giants

in the foreground but of radio
a source, emission
from ionized gas and a concentration

of a mass of stars equivalent
to two million suns. They shed some light

on human history, a consolation knowing
those old settlers of the new world headed
in the right direction. We're going there brother

one way or another
when the Big Banger
be it He or She or Whatever

inhales. Is that 'A' confirmation
of Zukofsky's source and range, he on top
of everything
                    a *Scientific American*

reader? Maybe he had back issues
in the can. For us unfortunate children
born on the way to Christmas these

make a more than perfect
gift, a combination
present: lives stacked under
the right stars. That future constellation

spoke first for Jansky hearing
its steady hiss, suggesting

we can guess who's resident
in Eden still. Oh yes, oh let's

be definite. In this
galaxy, our universe
one thing's forever central,
certain—an imaginative man

can be as readily lonely
in bed with his wife
as in homely contemplation

of Sagittarius A West.

### When I Heard the Learned Deconstructionist
*to Linda Kaufman*

When I heard the learned deconstructionist
hold forth upon the formlessness of love
but for literary artifice (the Frenchman
with the woman's voice, the feminist protesting
he had stolen hers, the redundancy

of gender) I looked about in the windowless
lecture theatre at the beautiful and singular
beings there, each discrete genetic

proposition, and heard in their tentative
laughter, unease

and determination

never to be taken for those fools believing
love's voices individual. Her shivering glissando
begun of ardent whisper in the family room
and hard breathing

must be Madonna soundtrack
or the university's

mere tonal variant
of all the flat cool lighting left—
the snowy hiss at the end
of the video, the steady-

state hum of the standby mode signal
profound beyond one's next articulation.

## A Clue

Outside through sunset
pulling nails from the old siding
I duck and make a run for it

a few yards to the edge
of the clearing dodging
the mosquito cloud
a second or two
to take a leak, look up. . .

I'd forgotten the new
moon amulet, silver
sliver of anchor
in the expansive

blue, clue
to my continuing

stance here, feet apart
planted

on deck in the earth's haul.

Anachronistic. Bitten.

## Acknowledgements

The poems in *Forecast* previously appeared in the publications listed below. I'm especially grateful these decades later to their editors/publishers/designers/printers who gave me and my early work context and community.

BOOKS & CHAPBOOKS
*Taking Place*, Talonbooks, Vancouver, 1971 (David Phillips, David Robinson, Gordon Fidler)
*AIR 18*, Airbooks, Vancouver, 1973 (Bertrand Lachance)
*Port of Entry*, Repository Press, Prince George, 1975 (John Harris)
*Love's Confidence*, Caledonia Writing Series, Prince George, 1976 (Barry McKinnon)
*Blossom: An Accompaniment*, Cobblestone Press, Vancouver, 1978 (Gerald Giampa, Martin Jensen)
*There Go the Cars*, Sesame Press, Windsor, 1978 (Eugene McNamara)
*An Arbitrary Dictionary*, Coach House Press, Toronto, 1984 (bp Nichol, Gordon Robertson)
*Rugosa*, Reference West/Hawthorne Society, Victoria, 1991 (Charles Lillard, Rhonda Batchelor)

PERIODICALS
*A is A* (Scott Calhoun)
*BC Monthly* (Gerry Gilbert)
*Canadian Forum* (Douglas Barbour)
*The Capilano Review* (Pierre Coupey)
*EVENT* (Dale Zieroth)
*ellipse* (Sharon Thesen)
*Fine Madness* (Louis Bergsagel)
*Geist* (Bryan Carson)
*Georgia Straight* (Stan Persky)
*Grain* (Caroline Heath)
*Iron II* (Sharon Fawcett, Brett Enemark)
*The Malahat Review* (Robin Skelton, Constance Rooke)
*PRISM International* (Richard Stevenson, Janis McKenzie)
*Repository* (John Harris)
*West Coast Review* (Charles Watts)
*WOT* (John Barton)

ANTHOLOGIES
*boundary2*, State University of New York, Binghamton, 1974 (eds. Margaret Atwood, Warren Tallman)
*Young North American Poets*, Spring Rain Press, Seattle, 1974 (eds. Karen and John Sollid)

*The Body*, Tatlow House, North Vancouver, 1979 (eds. David Phillips, Hope Anderson)

*Anthology of Magazine Verse & Yearbook of American Poetry*, Monitor Book Co., Beverly Hills, 1981

*A Labour of Love*, Polestar Press, Winlaw, 1989 (ed. Mona Fertig)

*A Verse Map of Vancouver*, Anvil Press, Vancouver, 2009 (ed. George McWhirter)

*One More Once*, CUE, North Vancouver, 2012 (ed. Jenny Penberthy)

BROADSHEETS & EPHEMERA

"Trellis," Caledonia Writing Series, 1975 (Barry McKinnon)

"An Empty Glass," Barbarian Press, 1981 (Crispin & Jan Elsted)

"Poem for the New World," High Ground, 1981

"Second Son," High Ground, 1983

"Sojourn," Coach House Press, 1984 (Tom Nethercott)

"One. Life," High Ground, 1985

KEITH SHAW

**John Pass**'s poems have appeared in magazines and anthologies in Canada, the US, the UK, Ireland and the Czech Republic. He is the author of nineteen books and chapbooks, most notably the quartet AT LARGE, comprised of *The Hour's Acropolis* (Harbour, 1991), *Radical Innocence* (Harbour, 1994), *Water Stair* (Oolichan Books, 2000)—shortlisted for the Governor General's Award—and *Stumbling in the Bloom* (Oolichan Books, 2005)—winner of the Governor General's Award. His most recent collection, *crawlspace*, published by Harbour in 2011, won the Dorothy Livesay Poetry Prize in 2012. He lives with his wife, writer Theresa Kishkan, near Sakinaw Lake on BC's Sunshine Coast.